The Purple Pill Workbook

God's Call for His Bride to Make Herself Ready

Robert E. Statham

Dedication

To all who long for God's best in their lives....

Copyright

The Purple Pill Workbook
God's call for His bride to make herself ready.

Copyright © 2018 Robert E. Statham

All rights reserved under International Copyright Law. No part of this workbook, text or cover, may be reproduced without written permission from the publisher.

Published by GooseBear Press
www.GooseBear.com
Editor: Allesa Statham
Cover design, media, and content layout by GB Media

Unless noted all scripture taken from the Holy Bible, NEW INTERNATIONAL VERSION ®, NIV ® Copyright © 1973, 1978, 1984, 2011 by Biblica, Inc. ® Used by permission. All rights reserved worldwide.

To contact the author about speaking at your conference or church, please contact via email rob@robstatham.com or social media @RobertEStatham.

All GooseBear Press books are available at Christian bookstores and distributors worldwide.

ISBN: 978-0-9996959-6-8
Library of Congress Control Number: 2018914753

Copyright

Printed in the United States of America for distribution worldwide.

Table of Contents

Preface............................ 9
Getting Started.................. 11
One: Introduction............. 17
Two: The Mirror.............. 21
Three: The Enemy........... 27
Four: The Call................ 33
Five: Inside Out.............. 39
Six: The Invisible Wall...... 43
Seven: The Maze............ 47
Eight: The Process............ 51
Nine: Your Purpose.......... 57
Ten: His Order................. 63
Eleven: His Kingdom.......... 69
Declarations of Life............. 75
Author Page......................83

Preface

WORDS,
Create pictures in your mind,
Imprints upon your heart,
And ultimately determine your destiny.

The purpose for this workbook is to assist, in group or individual study, application of God's heart while reading "The Purple Pill."

We are living on the precipice of the greatest revival the world has ever seen and it is coming through people, like you, hearing the Spirit of the Lord calling them into their divine destiny. Before divine destiny comes divine alignment. Life comes as we position ourselves to receive and fulfill God's purpose for our individual lives. God's sets you free, matures you, anoints you, and then leads you to impart what He's given you to the people around you.

> Words are the hallmark of humanity.
> We use words to build up or tear down.
> Words create our future; good or bad.
> Words have the power of life and death.
> Choose words of life.

Preface

My prayer for you over this 12 week journey is that you will partner with God's Spirit and allow Him reveal the loving plans He has for you. I pray you tap-in to the unforced rhythms of His grace as you waltz with Him and discover a deeper, more intimate relationship with the God who thought of you before the foundations of the world. His thoughts and purpose for you will be revealed as you trust Him and apply the truths of His word that are highlighted by the Spirit of Jesus. He has plans to prosper you and longs to fulfill His loving plans. May God break every chain the enemy's tried to entangle you with. May He grant you the Spirit of wisdom and revelation as He opens the eyes of your heart. May you realize the incomparably great power He has for you, that you are a king on this earth ushering in His Kingdom for His glory, and your blessing.

In Jesus name, Amen!

Getting Started

It is time for all of us to discover the riches of God's grace He has hidden in our divine purpose. This equally applies to the individual and, of course, His bride, the body of Christ.
This is a guide to put the concepts learned from the book, "The Purple Pill," into practice.

Intimacy always births revelation while building depth to your relationship with God and others. When relationships are strengthened then growth always follows.

Each workbook chapter will be set up in the following easy to follow format:

OVERVIEW Chapter
The overview will be a chapter summary of the book. This will aid in sparking one's memory of the highlights of the chapter.

TEACHING POINTS:
This will be a bulleted list of the main points of the chapter. The leader of the discussion should use these to highlight the main points.

DISCUSSION:

Getting Started

This consists of a bulleted list to aid in group discussions. Often a group needs a subject or statement presented to help prime the discussion. This list highlights areas to probe and help strengthen the teaching points.

ACTIVATION:
We must put knowledge into practice to reap the rewards God has for us. The activation is a simple exercise to put teaching concepts into practice.

SCRIPTURE REFERENCES
Each scripture that is referred to is printed here for quick reference.

My heartfelt desire is this workbook will give you practical counsel to apply the concepts learned from the book.

I pray God's grace will meet your every need and you will side with Him against the world and your flesh. Pray with me, "I will partner with your Spirit to speak words of life. I ask you to impart your loving plans for my life. Plans to prosper me, to give me a hope, and good future. May you break every chain the enemy's tried to entangle me with. Help me take my place, and play my part as You usher in the greatest revival ever. May your Kingdom come, your will be done, right here and everywhere You lead me on earth, just as it is in Heaven! Freedom, Love, Joy, and Peace chase me down and overtake me in abundance. Give me ears to hear and the Spirit of wisdom and revelation. Open the eyes of my heart. I want to know you better. I want

to know your heart for me and those around me.
Use me for your glory and my blessing.
   In Jesus name, Amen!"

Purple Pill Book Study

One

Introduction

WORDS,
Create pictures in your mind,
Imprints upon your heart,
And ultimately determine your destiny.

OVERVIEW Chapter 1 - Introduction
The book's purpose is to share words that help create God's picture of your life. The picture God paints in your mind is the beautiful thoughts and desires God has for you. The stumbling block to many comes because this wonderful picture does not line up with what's seen and perceived as reality. This wrestling match within must take place. The truth of God's word is challenging and taking to the mat the thoughts and beliefs we live by that have tried to stand against His loving will. As the truth washes over you like the waves at the seashore these words will leave an imprint on your heart. Once embraced above the five senses and the thoughts trying to stand against the knowledge of God the most wonderful picture in your heart will come into focus and you will see the beautiful destiny He has for you.
We serve a loving God that has a heart to redeem and restore the brokenness we find in our lives due to

sin, poor choices, and the work of our enemy the devil. We at times side with the very thing that is hurting us. Often realizing, far too late, that we are in a mess. Jesus loves to take our brokenness, heal, restore and glorify our Father in heaven. We are the beneficiary of a God who loves us more than we have ever realized and He wants to prove it to you.

This wonderful life comes by being in alignment with God to receive and fulfill His will, which is His purpose, for our lives. Living in His Kingdom showing yourself to be His disciple. Words are the catalyst to bring us into alignment. Change is on the horizon and it is good. We cannot continue to do what we have done in the past and expect change. We also cannot change for the sake of change and hope it brings positive change. We must be in alignment and led by the Spirit of God. When He highlights a needed change we must embrace it, for it is only there we walk in life and life in abundance.

We are living on the precipice of the **Greatest Revival the world has ever seen**, but few recognize it. Alignment is the key to ushering in this great move of God.

TEACHING POINTS:
- o   Our words have the power of life and death (Proverbs 18:21).
- o   Often we believe what we see is true, but if we see anything that doesn't agree with God's heart revealed through His word then it may be a fact but may not true. Truth is what God says; not what the we say, the world says, or anyone else.

- Romans 12 tells us to bless and not curse.

DISCUSSION:
- How are you (0-5,5 high) with the WORDS you speak? Are you quick to encourage, forgive, and speak words of hope? Share your rating and an example story that comes to mind.
- Before divine destiny comes divine alignment. Life comes as we position ourselves to receive and fulfill God's purpose for our individual lives.

ACTIVATION:
This week, **each day** ask God for the Spirit of wisdom and revelation & speak words with Kingdom purpose (READ EPHESIANS 1:17-20). Expect to "see" what God sees or to "see" something familiar in a new way. The brave ones be ready to share next week.

SCRIPTURE REFERENCES:
"The mouth of the righteous is a fountain of life."
    - Proverbs 10:11a

"Reckless words pierce like a sword, but the tongue of the wise brings healing."
    - Proverbs 12:18

"From the fruit of his lips a man enjoys good things."
    - Proverbs 13:2a

"He who guards his lips guards his life, but he who speaks rashly will come to ruin."
    -Proverbs 13:3

Introduction

"The tongue has the power of life and death, and those who love it will eat its fruit."
    -Proverbs 18:21

"Bless those who persecute you; bless and do not curse."
    - Romans 12:14

"For I know the plans I have for you," declares the LORD , "plans to prosper you and not to harm you, plans to give you hope and a future."
    - Jeremiah 29:11

I keep asking that the God of our Lord Jesus Christ, the glorious Father, may give you the **Spirit of wisdom and revelation**, so that you may **know him** better. I pray also that the **eyes of your heart may be enlightened in order that you may know the hope to which he has called you**, the riches of his glorious inheritance in the saints, and his incomparably **great power for us who believe**. That power is like the working of his mighty strength, which he exerted in Christ when he raised him from the dead and seated him at his right hand in the heavenly realms.
    - Ephesians 1:17-20 (*emphasis added*)

Two

The Mirror

"No man has a chance to enjoy permanent success until he begins to look in a mirror for the real cause of all his mistakes."
- Napoleon Hill.

OVERVIEW Chapter 2 - The Mirror
As Christians examine themselves in the mirror of truth a devastating chasm appears. The Lord Jesus Christ left us with an expectation to bear much fruit. A sobering assessment reveals little fruit. **What has gripped the body of Christ that keeps us paralyzed on the sidelines of life?** The picture that comes into view is one of isolation and cannibalism. In our quest to build the church our relationship within His body is strained. Jesus said he will build the church, and we are to make disciples. Jesus did this through relationship for three and half years with 12 men. Discipleship is not a class Thursday evening, it is real, face to face, heart to heart, relationship.

God is stirring believers igniting the desire deep within

their hearts for real relationship, and calling them into alignment. The hunger inside is fruit of the stirring in their spirits to rise to His call.   God is bringing His Kingdom of light right here on earth as it is in heaven. He is doing it through His people; through relationship. He is stirring you now to fulfill His divine call on your life for you, your family, your city, and your nation. **The result will be the greatest revival in the world has ever witnessed.**

The dilemma is you may see the problems but how can one person make a difference? The first step is to look in the mirror to see an accurate reflection. The mirror is His Word. Individually and corporately we will be transformed into a bride without spot or wrinkle, ready to meet the Bridegroom.

Wisdom equips us to reign in life. We cannot afford any thoughts that are not His. Opinions don't work, yours or others - we need His opinions. Guilt, Shame, Regret, and Bitterness cripple. Our bodies respond to us - mentally, emotionally, and physically.
People live together forming the culture, church or work, and somehow lose the understanding how to effect change outside of themselves for the good. It's not readily apparent to everyone that the reason things go wrong is because they played a part in it. The critical word here is "part."

How does this apply to you, our church, and our country? Here's the bombshell; **We need to change.** Mark Twain once said, "The only person who likes change is a wet baby." Today, I encourage you to be open to new things - God has new things in store for you. When we are not willing to change, we wear a rut in life holding on to what God did in the past instead of changing and moving forward into what God is doing now. We cannot continue to do what we have been doing and hope for different results. The thought that unity is going to come by all the other silo's (churches) watching as your individual church transforms the city is plainly wrong. It is evidenced by a lack of fruit. The obvious fruit of those beliefs is disunity and pride. Pride that our church is better than the one down the street. Those thoughts are not coming from God's heart.

We are are a reflection of our value system. Our lives and our church reflect what we value. We read Acts 2:38-41 where the believers devoted themselves to the Apostle's teaching, fellowship, the breaking of bread, and prayer. Their numbers grew daily! This reflects their value system.
Most, not all for there is always a remnant, have pursued church as being Sunday morning. This consists of coming together with little or no time to truly fellowship and share what is happening in our lives - good and bad. Isolation. The deception of isolation is that it brings protection (garden of eden).

Relationship is reflected in what Jesus valued. It is also the purpose of communion. Jesus ate with sinners and tax collectors (Mt 9:10), but He did not sin with them. It was through relationship that the love of God resonated in their hearts to heed His invitation into relationship and enter the Kingdom of God.

Jesus said a wise man hears the word and puts it into practice (Mt 7:24). Others only listen and get swept away by the storms of life.
Money is a quick and easy way to see where our heart is. We often get sidetracked by the issue of money. We know God loves a cheerful giver, unfortunately most are not cheerful, but give out of a sense of obligation. The fruit of giving out of obligation is emptiness. You'd be better off to not give. God doesn't need your money. He loves you and wants your heart because only then will you be set free and happy. He knows you cannot serve two masters or you will die (Mt 6:24).

We live in the world and take a couple hours Sunday to honor God, thinking a bath (washed with the water of the word) once a week is working. Waiting and saying we're ready to get serious when we see God really move. Until then, we'll give a little and wait. Confused why well over 80% of Millennials want nothing to do with today's Church? Why kids are lost, hurt, and dying? Why God doesn't do something? He has done EVERYTHING. He has sat down and is waiting for His enemies to be made a footstool. **We wait on God while He waits on us to believe Him and act like it.**
Think of the Israelites in the days of Moses. There was the land of Egypt, or how it was. The promised land, or how it should be. And the desert between the two - the land of transition. This is a fabulous land to cross through, but a terrible land to settle in. God's heart is to renew your life to move into the promised land.

The Purple Pill Book Study

TEACHING POINTS:
- God works through relationships. He uses people; Adam & Eve, Noah, Abraham, Joseph, Moses, David, Solomon, and you.
- The mirror of truth will equip us and align us to be knit in God's tapestry for the world to see His glory. We are a part of the body, not the whole thing.
- "Therefore everyone who hears these words of mine and puts them into practice is like a wise man who built his house on the rock." - Matthew 7:24

DISCUSSION:
- Last week you were asked to pray every day for the Spirit of wisdom and revelation & sow words with Kingdom purpose. How did you do?
- Eyes are useless when the mind is blind; the only way things improve is to see the need for change.
- Step 1 is gaze into the mirror of truth to see an accurate reflection. Fun house mirrors, like the world's wisdom, distort what we see. God's word gives us an accurate reflection of ourselves.
- "The only person who likes change is a wet baby." -Mark Twain
- Relationship is key to partner with God and the purpose of communion. Hiding and thinking if people don't see then you're ok is not ok.

ACTIVATION:

The Mirror

Commune with God when you wake up. Spend 5 minutes meditating on God. Not reading, Not praying, just meditating. Then pray and ask God to show you what's on His heart. Write down what comes to mind. Find the scripture(s) that help and line up with what you're hearing, then ACT on it. It is critical that we act on God's word and not merely listen to it. Be ready to share next week.

SCRIPTURE REFERENCES:
"Do not merely listen to the word, and so deceive yourselves. Do what it says."
- James 1:22

"The weapons we fight with are not the weapons of the world. On the contrary, they have divine power to demolish strongholds. We demolish arguments and every pretension that sets itself up against the knowledge of God, and we take captive every thought to make it obedient to Christ."
- 2 Corinthians 10:4-5

"No one can serve two masters. Either you will hate the one and love the other, or you will be devoted to the one and despise the other. You cannot serve both God and money."
- Matthew 6:24

Three

The Enemy

> "OUR greatest fear should not be failing, but rather succeeding at things that don't really matter..."
> - Francis Chan

<u>OVERVIEW Chapter 3 - The Enemy</u>
Out battle is against spiritual forces of evil in the heavenly realms, yet few understand how to recognize the battle and even fewer understand how to respond. Evil always attacks a weakness with intent to deceive, in order that we might give up a strength. It is our nature to build fortified defenses using our strengths. Unfortunately, the enemy doesn't attack our strengths, but bypasses them and targets our weakness. The enemy's intent is to separate and create a lone silo of believers. Our strength is in our Godly relationships, in the aggregate of the body. One individual silo is vulnerable. One example would be a Pastor tempted with an illicit relationship. His weakness in turn gives the enemy entry to destroy the unity of the church. The reaction is usually according to feelings and not truth. This leads to walking according to our flesh which is out of order. Christians not walking according to the Spirit, are Christians

The Enemy

building on sand. Thus, crippling and anesthetizing the church.

TEACHING POINTS:
- The simplest tactic of darkness is to distract us with being busy so we do not invest in what brings us life and glorifies our Father in heaven.
- The bible reveals (2 Corinthians 4:4) is that Satan has blinded the minds of unbelievers.
- Religion takes a hold of God's truth and twists it just enough that it actually brings death. The Pharisees had the very same ancient manuscripts that Jesus had.
- How can I not fall into the same trap? Well, Jesus was motivated by LOVE. God is Love (1 John 4:8).
- The same water Jesus offered the woman at the well resides in you if you are born again and sealed with the Holy Spirit, BUT it will never flow out of you without love. You get wet first, then you can share it. It flows by love, not by want.
- Love your neighbor as <u>yourself</u> (Mt 22:39).

DISCUSSION:
- How did you do 5 minutes communing with God? What did God highlight? Share?
- Busy and Effective are not synonyms.
- Unbelief is blindness. Evil always attacks a weakness with intent to deceive, in order that we might give up a strength.
- Religion takes a hold of God's truth and twists it just enough that it actually brings death. The Pharisees had the very same ancient

manuscripts Jesus had.
- The moment the enemy entices us to act for any other reason than **love** then we have fertile soil for a spirit of religion to grow. The outside appearance becomes the focus, wrongly thinking this has any effect on our heart.
- People flocked to love, not a form of religion.
- We must love each other before we can love the world.
- Yearning for life in a desert of religion the enemy tells us the fault lies outside of us, and therefore we cannot change it. It's their fault. They need to change.
- God's motive is love because God is love.
- He is love and His church is the ecclesia—His called-out ones, His government on the earth. Called out to love and bring life to a hurting, dying world.

ACTIVATION:
Read this daily (out loud):
I walk in the footsteps of Jesus - I walk in love. I don't just read the greatest commandment, I actually love the Lord with all of my heart, mind, soul, and strength. I love my family. I love my neighbors. I love at work, church, the grocery store and anywhere else the Spirit of God leads me. I live my life today for Him, I look forward to the day I am face to face with my Lord and Savior Jesus and hear, "Well done! You have been a good and faithful servant. Come your reward awaits you."

SCRIPTURE REFERENCES:

The Enemy

"The god of this age has blinded the minds of unbelievers, so that they cannot see the light of the gospel that displays the glory of Christ, who is the image of God."
- 2 Corinthians 4:4

"Do not revile the king even in your thoughts,
    or curse the rich in your bedroom,
because a bird in the sky may carry your words,
    and a bird on the wing may report what you say."
- Ecclesiastes 10:20

"The tongue has the power of life and death,
    and those who love it will eat its fruit."
- Proverbs 18:21

"A wise man's heart guides his mouth, and his lips promote instruction."
-Proverbs 16:23

"But I tell you that everyone will have to give account on the day of judgment for every empty word they have spoken."
- Matthew 12:36

"If one part suffers, every part suffers with it; if one part is honored, every part rejoices with it."
- 1 Corinthians 12:26

"Whoever does not love does not know God, because God is love."
- 1 John 4:8

"Jesus replied: 'Love the Lord your God with all your heart and with all your soul and with all your mind.' This is the first and greatest commandment. And the second is like it: 'Love your neighbor as yourself.' All the Law and the Prophets hang on these two commandments."
- Matthew 22:37-40

Four

The Call

ALIGNMENT

> "Those who cling to worthless idols forfeit the grace that could be theirs."
> -Jonah 2:8

OVERVIEW Chapter 4 - The Call
We must align ourselves with God and quit forfeiting His powerful Grace. In Jonah 2:8 we find a profound truth, "Those who cling to worthless idols forfeit the grace that could be theirs." When we see what God sees - truth - then we are walking in His light, but when you see what God does not see - a lie - then you are in trouble. Out of order, out of balance, and clinging to worthless idols. Any beliefs you place over and before what God says is an idol and steals His grace from your life. Revival only comes through alignment with God. All revivals start with people aligning themselves with God's truth. Not one started with some outpouring of the Spirit like raindrops falling out of the sky that you have no control over. God meets you where you're at and then calls you to follow Him - Align yourself with what He is doing.

The Call

Purpose
"The two most important days of your life are the day you were born and the day you find out why."
-Mark Twain

You can do anything, but you cannot do everything. Choose to do what God already planned for you, then you will discover your purpose.

What We set our Eyes On
"When you take your eyes off your nakedness and failure, insight provides identity, and foresight provides destiny, which are the two keys to living a prophetic lifestyle."
- Kim Clement

We are not limited to only our natural sight. With natural eyes, we see the world all around us. The second way we see is with our soul through insight or our mind's eyes. The third way we "see" is the best way - we see with our spirit. This is described as the eyes of faith or foresight. **We see what God sees.**
You must believe and act on what God Almighty has told you over what you see, what your friends say, over what you might even think! God's word is true and until you stand up and act on what you believe, not on what you see, you will never walk in God's abundant life of faith.

CALL TO ACT - ALIGN YOURSELF
Law of diminishing Intent - the longer you

wait to act on inspiration, the more likely you will not act.

TEACHING POINTS:
- We see a reflection of our self in everyone we know. People are often negative towards others because they're negative towards themselves.
- Revival comes when we align ourselves with God just as Nineveh did.
- Purpose; God had you in His mind before the foundation of the world (Ephesians 1:4). Those thoughts are His intent for you (Jer 29:11) or your purpose.
- He created you to walk by faith. Without faith you cannot please God.
- You can do anything, but you cannot do everything.
- Law of diminishing Intent - the longer you wait to act on inspiration, the more likely you will not act.
- Law of diminishing Intent - the longer you wait to act on inspiration, the more likely you will not act.

DISCUSSION:
- Experiences from last week's declaration. Share?
- Beliefs you place over and before what God says is an idol and steals His grace from your life.
- The wrong image is only replaced through the

The Call

- truth of the living Word.
  - Revival only comes through alignment with God. Ezekiel 37 and Jonah.
  - Your God given gifts and call reveal your purpose.
  - You can do anything, but you cannot do everything. "If you want to destroy a man's vision, give him two." -Andrew Wommack
  - Live by sight, insight, and foresight to live by Faith.

ACTIVATION:
Alignment. This activation hurts so good. Bad beliefs lie hidden until confronted with the truth. God does this gently yet firmly. We often recognize these moments by experiencing frustration/aggravation with a teaching/truth that contradicts our heart. A truth that rubs you the wrong way. This is actually good. Prayerfully list a belief the Spirit is highlighting that you place before God. If you're brave be ready to share it next week. Ask God for grace to lose distractions and live by faith. Spirit first, then mind (soul), and body.

SCRIPTURE REFERENCES:
"Those who cling to worthless idols forfeit the grace that could be theirs."
-Jonah 2:8

Ezekiel 37 Valley of dry bones.

"For he chose us in him before the creation of the world to be holy and blameless in his sight."

- Ephesians 1:4

"For I know the plans I have for you," declares the LORD , "plans to prosper you and not to harm you, plans to give you hope and a future."
- Jeremiah 29:11

"And without faith it is impossible to please God, because anyone who comes to him must believe that he exists and that he rewards those who earnestly seek him."
-Hebrews 11:6

"I hate those who cling to worthless idols; I trust in the Lord."
Psalms 31:6

Five

Inside Out

"WORDS may show a man's wit, but actions his meaning."
- Benjamin Franklin

OVERVIEW Chapter 5 - Inside Out
God graciously reveals gaps between what we say we believe and what we do, which is what we really believe. The beginning of God peeling layers of our hearts. Our behavior is the servant of our beliefs. Our minds can actually be blind to ourselves. We judge others by their actions and ourselves by our intentions. At the onset of taking a stand, spiritual or otherwise, human beings tend to say the right things. Declaring the truth is easy, but beliefs are tested as we walk through life. The trials and trouble of life quickly put our words to the test. Our behavior confirms or denies our utterance. God reveals one thing at a time. If we ignore it then He patiently shows us again. If we acknowledge it and align ourselves with Him we grow. Little by little, like one starfish at a time, we are set free.
Just as David was able to question who this is that would defy the armies of the living God and then run at a giant, defeating him with a sling and a stone.

Inside Out

Every man in that army had the same opportunity and said the same thing about the Philistines, but when tested, they cowered. The declaration shared in this chapter will help anyone change from the inside out.

TEACHING POINTS:
- The author had a "who's my neighbor" moment exposing the duplicity of his heart. He hated it in others and changed when he saw it in himself.
- God always starts with you. The speck in your eye is remedied before the plank in another's.
- "The mouth of the righteous is a fountain of life..." -Proverbs 10:11a
- Declaring God's truths over your life changes everything. It brings us into alignment with God and our lives bear abundant fruit.

DISCUSSION:
- Who wants to share a "bad belief" from last week's assignment that God is uprooting?
- Testimony of "who's my neighbor." The onion started to get peeled that day.
- We judge others by their actions and ourselves by our intentions.
- Peter was used to change the world, but first Peter was changed.
- You are the starfish. It's just one and it starts with you.
- Inside Out is about a relationship with God. The closer you get to Him the easier it is to declare His truth over your life in faith.
- The truth is, we speak what we believe.

ACTIVATION:
Read the declaration out loud every day. Watch God peel the onion of your beliefs. The Holy Spirit will graciously highlight some truths you confess but do not put into practice.

SCRIPTURE REFERENCES:
"From the fruit of their mouth a person's stomach is filled; with the harvest of their lips they are satisfied. The tongue has the power of life and death, and those who love it will eat its fruit."
-Proverbs 18: 20-21

"By faith we understand that the universe was formed at God's command, so that what is seen was not made out of what was visible."
-Hebrews 11:3

"Then God said, 'Let us make man in our image, in our likeness, and let them rule over the fish of the sea and the birds of the air, over the livestock, over all the earth, and over all the creatures that move along the ground.'"
-Genesis 1:26

"The mouth of the righteous is a fountain of life..."
-Proverbs 10:11a

"From the fruit of their mouth a person's stomach is filled;
with the harvest of their lips they are satisfied.
The tongue has the power of life and death,

Inside Out

and those who love it will eat its fruit."
- Proverbs 18:20-21

Six

The Invisible Wall

"LESSONS in life will be repeated until they are learned."
-Frank Sonnenburg

OVERVIEW Chapter 6 - The Invisible Wall
Often people treat circumstances as the fences of life. They run into one then turn and go along with it, as if running into a fence in a field. All the time wishing, thinking, even praying the circumstance will change. The wise ones realize the circumstances they are faced with are revealing who they are and, this is critical, **what needs to change** in them. You change for two reasons. Either you learn enough that you want to, or you've been hurt enough that you have to.

When life seems to be clicking along just fine and you crash face first into an invisible wall of life. Nose bloody, dusting yourself off and wondering what just happened. You are faced with a choice. You can hit the wall again or you can go in another direction. <u>The wall is simply a trial testing what we believe.</u> There is only one reason to go towards that wall again. That is because you know that wall, that obstacle is between

The Invisible Wall

you and God's plans for you. If you do not know that then, confused, you go in the path of least resistance, which is also the wrong direction. This repeated, soon you find yourself in a dry and weary land where there is no water - but you have lots of company.

Wandering you beg God to do something. He has in fact done everything, but you now suffer from spiritual blindness that comes from unbelief. The way to the promised land is by discovering your purpose.

The living God always works from the inside out. He begins with our heart first. Normally, we want Him to change our circumstances, all of the outward things we continually face. When our heart is completely His, things begin to change externally.

Think about David and put yourself in his shoes as he was watching over sheep and a lion shows up. I would run away from the test until I knew and believed in my heart that God's will was on the other side of me killing that lion. He saw the lion as a test of his faith, not a day to die.

The enemy always offers a short cut which appeals to our natural man as a way out of the uncomfortable circumstance, but is fundamentally wrong because you are putting yourself and your thinking above God. Remember we are supposed to serve Him only. **A short cut tests if we believe what we say.** Because your actions show what you believe.

TEACHING POINTS:
- A wall is a test you were born to pass.
- God is not trying to teach us a formula for success, He is trying to teach us obedience is success, because he tells us only what is best for

us.
- A short cut is the way out that appeals to our natural nature, but is fundamentally wrong because you are putting yourself and your thinking above God.
- Jesus told us to love the Lord our God with **all of our heart**.
- In Psalms 23 God is preparing a table for you in the presence of your enemies. Problems weren't vanquished, God worked in the midst of them.

DISCUSSION:
- Growth without change is impossible, to go to the next level you must change.
- How do you change? Learn or hurt.
- Tests expose our hearts. It is not human nature to run at a lion like David did. David put himself aside to serve God.
- God works from the inside out. Normally, we want Him to change our circumstances, but often He works within our hearts before we see outward change.
- Short-cuts short-circuit God's good, perfect, and pleasing plan.

ACTIVATION:
Ask the Holy Spirit to reveal a circumstance, or test, in your life where He is trying to teach you and help you through it, not avoid it.

SCRIPTURE REFERENCES:
"And we know that in all things God works for the

good of those who love him, who have been called according to his purpose."
- Romans 8:28

"Jesus said to him, 'Away from me, Satan! For it is written: 'Worship the Lord your God, and serve him only.'"
- Matthew 4:10

"For you, O God, tested us; you refined us like silver."
- Psalms 66:10

"The crucible for silver and the furnace for gold, but the Lord tests the heart."
- Proverbs 17:3

"You prepare a table before me
in the presence of my enemies.
You anoint my head with oil;
my cup overflows."
- Psalms 23:5

Seven

The Maze

> "WHEN written in Chinese the word 'crisis' is composed of two characters, one represents danger and the other represents opportunity."
> - John F. Kennedy

OVERVIEW Chapter 7 - The Maze
Socrates, the renown philosopher who lived about 400 years before Christ, said, "Beware the barrenness of a busy life." The routine is what forms your thoughts and attitudes. The thoughts and attitudes make up who you are and what you do.
The trap in this is the daily routine that is developed. It is dangerous, but it is also an opportunity. We try to avoid the trap by imitating what's worked before or follow someone else's directions to avoid the invisible walls. This sounds like a great idea and it would be except the invisible walls are actually part of a maze and each person's path is different. We think a routine or discipline will keep us safe from the enemy's trap. In reality, it is part of the trap, a detour from God's best for you. I love routine and discipline but do not ever let those things rule over relationship. **Relationship keeps us from blindly wearing a rut.**
There is only one way to navigate this invisible maze

we call life and that's listening to the only one who sees it, loves us, and longs to spend time with us.

Every test may result in discomfort to our selfish nature or carnal nature - most people call this pain. An athlete beats his body in training so as to compete to win the race. The body screams but the spirit leads. The teacher is always quiet during the test. The teacher cannot pass the test for you or you won't grow in your understanding, confidence, or calling in life. The enemy comes with thoughts that God's will shouldn't cause pain. This is a lie. Throughout His word we read that God tests our hearts. Our faith will be tested. In fact, Jesus said you will have trouble in this world, but take heart for He has overcome the world.

TEACHING POINTS:
- A busy routine can be a problem, why?
- Relationship with God keeps us from the ruts of life. The invisible maze we call life can be navigated only by listening to the only One who sees it, loves us, and has good plans for us.
- Who is on the throne of your heart?
- The body screams but the spirit leads. The discomfort to our selfish nature yields to the joy of our spirit when yielded to Him.
- God has a great plan and wants to prosper you, and use you to be a blessing everywhere you go. To do that you must believe Him. You must trust Him and grow in Him. **You must see your purpose is through the test opposing you**, THEN you will stand up and walk in victory.

DISCUSSION:

- Who would like to share a circumstance or test the Spirit has highlighted for the activation last week?
- Worship is your daily routine demonstrating what rules your heart.
- God tests us to show us our hearts. He is producing the character of His Son in you. To navigate this invisible maze, we must listen to the Master. I am asking who is on the throne of your heart when nobody is watching.
- Your struggles are the very thing that you need to strengthen you for life ahead.
- God is doing a work that will shape eternity. He is calling you to play your part.
- You have been designed for this moment and His purpose.

ACTIVATION:
Are you willing to pursue His purpose for your life in spite of temporary pain and find intimate relationship with your Creator? Tell Him in prayer and show Him in actions.

SCRIPTURE REFERENCES:
Luke 4 Testing of Jesus

"And David inquired of the LORD , 'Shall I pursue this raiding party? Will I overtake them?'
'Pursue them,' he answered. 'You will certainly overtake them and succeed in the rescue.'"
- 1 Samuel 30:8

"He said to his servants, 'Stay here with the donkey

The Maze

while I and the boy go over there. We will worship and then we will come back to you.'"
- Genesis 22: 5

Eight

The Process

YOUR **Response to the Test**

In school, we learn lessons before the test, in life, we take the test before we learn the lesson.

OVERVIEW Chapter 8 - The Process
There is a God ordained process for responding to trials and the testing of our heart. The steps to the process include letting go of bias and any blame. This is critical for anyone to begin to understand His will, not ours. The next step is to gather and accurately analyze all of the truth that has manifested around you in one form of evidence or another. People are certainly critical to this process because God always uses people. Don't think for one moment that any individual is able to sit alone in a closet and grow into the person God has called them to be. It is not good for man to be alone. After seeing the truth in light of your circumstances then His direction will be obvious, and you will be well on your way to fulfilling your destiny.
  Change - Renew your mind, think differently.

Bias and Blame.

> "For since the creation of the world God's invisible qualities—his eternal power and divine nature—have been clearly seen, being understood from what has been made, so that people are without excuse."
> - Romans 1:20

Bias is like a kaleidoscope - it completely changes the true picture. In fact, bias blinds. **Blame and bias keep you from ever seeing the truth.** Those who do not properly fear the Lord cannot detect their wrong thinking (Ps 36:2).

Evidence.

> The world looks for formulas. God looks for relationships.

Evidence is all around us. Immerse yourself in truth. Our enemy is bias. We have already made up our minds, in other words you can't see what is actually there – you only see what you think is there. People and relationships are critical to this process.

The Purple Pill Book Study

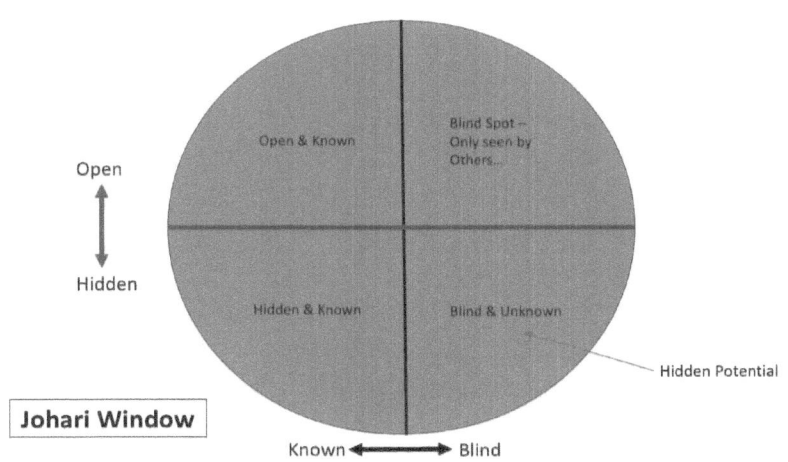

Revelation

The final, and liberating, step is to look at yourself in light of the evidence. The answer you find to this question is shocking:

> What is it about the way I am that contributed to this?

When you honestly answer this and others confirm your revelation you will experience freedom to a greater degree than you've experienced before. You will feel like doing a back-flip. The end result of this exercise is you think differently.

TEACHING POINTS:
- Without change we will never get better results.
- Bias blinds. When we blame we effectively turn our brain off and do not consider the evidence.
- God is truth and He uses the truth to lead us, but we must see it.

The Process

- Trusted relationships help you see what you cannot see.
- We all have blind spots (Johari window).
- Bless and do not curse. This means we are called to speak what God's thinking about people, not what we may see.
- If you live by faith you will see what God sees - you will see it with your heart, then you will see it with your eyes. First spirit, then natural.
- **God's greatest desire is not to expose your sin, but to expose His goodness.** He wants to set you free and let you walk according to His purpose.

DISCUSSION:
- CHANGE: you will never build a skyscraper by yourself.
- Bias is like a kaleidoscope - it completely changes the true picture. In fact, bias blinds. **Blame and bias keep you from ever seeing the truth.**
- Evidence is the truth surrounding us.
- Other people see what you cannot see. When you trust people, they help keep you honest.
- Bless and do not curse.
- Revelation is seeing with the eyes of faith. It is seeing what God sees.

ACTIVATION:
Ask the Holy Spirit to knit you into godly relationships built on His love. He will reveal a "blind spot" if you are willing to hear it. Remember He uses people.

SCRIPTURE REFERENCES:
"For since the creation of the world God's invisible qualities - his eternal power and divine nature - have been clearly seen, being understood from what has been made, so that men are without excuse."
-Romans 1:20

"Faithful are the wounds of a friend...."
- Proverbs 27:6a

"Bless those who persecute you; bless and do not curse."
- Romans 12:14

"All a man's ways seem innocent to him, but motives are weighed by the Lord."
-Proverbs 16:2

In his own eyes he flatters himself too much to detect or hate his sin.
- Psalms 36:2

"Do not conform any longer to the pattern of this world, but be transformed by the renewing of your mind. Then you will be able to test and approve what **God's will is--his good, pleasing and perfect will**."
- Romans 12:2 (emphasis added)

Nine

Your Purpose

> "For I know the plans I have for you," declares the LORD, "plans to prosper you and not to harm you, plans to give you hope and a future."
> - Jeremiah 29:11

OVERVIEW Chapter 9 - Your Purpose
Mark Twain once said, "The two most important days of your life are the day you were born and the day you find out why." The day you find out why you were born is the day you discover your purpose. It is the day the dreams in God's heart concerning you are made known to you. **You can do anything, but you cannot do everything.** Choose to do what God has for you. He is calling you to play a part in shaping eternity. Understanding your purpose and the process used to guide you is what places you in the right place at the right time doing the right thing - Order is restored to your life. A harvest is reaped in due season.
Remember destiny and purpose is more than a matter of what we *do* on our journey. It is a matter of who God says we already *are*, before we do anything or go anywhere we must be grounded in our heavenly identity.

Your Purpose

The path of life is a narrow way. Taking that path our purpose is unveiled. One does not find their purpose like a lost set of keys, rather it is a process. God will test you for the purposes of promoting you to a greater level of influence and to a greater level of maturity.

Whether you know your purpose or not you must enroll in God's higher education program. There is a path He has for you to follow that leads to life abundantly. Don't leave your destiny to chance. Don't try to fulfill your destiny in your own strength, for you are helpless without Him. This is about your relationship, your walk with God. This isn't about what you do by yourself or what He does for you by yourself.

The desire knit into all of our hearts is to fulfill our destiny, God's perfect plan for us. That is where we find the path of life.

Today, if $1,000,000.00 were deposited into your bank account, what would change?

What you do is proof of why you do it. If you work for food, then when you're full you will have no desire to work. If you work to feed the desires knit in your heart, then you will never do anything else and you'll do it with a smile.

The questions you need to answer by asking your Creator are:

What are you good at?

What do you love to do?

Why do you do what you do? "Why" is a loaded question in a small three-letter package. Think about what drives you, what inspires you, and what motivates you?

Prayerfully stare at these questions until you have

answers.

In John 14 Jesus shares His life *shows* He loves the Father. His "why" is love. Our "why" is also love. When it isn't then we quickly recognize that dry and weary place that so many people live in.

When you are in your purpose, that thing you were created for, you are not innovating something, or inventing something. You are simply revealing and discovering what has already been scripted by God before He created the foundations of the earth.

TEACHING POINTS:
- Purpose is "what" God's called you to do. Your gifts and talents are "how" to do it.
- Life is a journey and your purpose is unveiled as you walk on the path of life. (Ps 16:11)
- Fundamental daily practices are the training ground God chooses to mature you for the purpose of promotion to a greater level of influence.
- Each trial conquered ends with you being more like Him. An increase in the fruit of the Spirit. **Greater intimacy in your relationship and walk with God.**
- Today, if $1,000,000.00 were deposited into your bank account, what would change?
- What are you good at? What do you love to do? Why do you do what you do? **Prayerfully spend time pondering these questions until you have answers.**

DISCUSSION:
- You can do anything, but you cannot do

Your Purpose

- everything.
- "What" you are called to do will reveal your purpose. Not an easy question unless you tap into your Creator's thoughts and intents.
- Life is a journey and your purpose is unveiled as you walk on the path of life. (Ps 16:11)
- Your daily practices are the training grounds of life. Promotion and greater influence results from living what we've heard daily.
- **This is about your relationship, your walk with God.**
- Happiness is awesome, but it never should drive your life. It should be a byproduct of your life's choices.
- Today, if $1,000,000.00 were deposited into your bank account, what would change?
- What are you good at? What do you love to do? Why do you do what you do?

ACTIVATION:
Decide right now it is time to change! Declare, "Father, I am at your service. I want to enroll in your education program. Reveal why you have made me - what is my purpose? Prepare me to walk in it - spirit, soul, and body. I choose you, your love, your will over me. I trust you. I praise you. I thank you. May your glory shine through me today and every day. In Jesus name, Amen!" Mark this day in your journal, for today everything changes.

SCRIPTURE REFERENCES:
"You have made known to me the path of life; you will fill me with joy in your presence, with eternal pleasures

at your right hand." - Psalms 16:11

"For he chose us in him before the creation of the world to be holy and blameless in his sight."
- Ephesians 1:4

"Then you will call on me and come and pray to me, and I will listen to you. You will seek me and find me when you seek me with all your heart. I will be found by you," declares the Lord."
- Jeremiah 29:12

"Where the Spirit of the Lord is there is liberty."
- 2 Corinthians 3:17

"The Lord will fulfill his purpose for me your love, O Lord, endures forever."
- Psalms 138:8

Ten

His Order

His Order

> "As long as the earth endures,
> seedtime and harvest,
> cold and heat,
> summer and winter,
> day and night
> will never cease."
> -Genesis 8:22

OVERVIEW Chapter 10 - His Order
First the spirit then the natural. This is the order of creation, in fact, you could say this is the order of all things. There is a God ordained order in all of creation. As long as the earth endures, seedtime and harvest, cold and heat, summer and winter, day and night will never cease. The right action at the wrong time or the right action out of sequence leads to barrenness. If you plant seed and then plow you sabotage your own harvest. Seed planted in Winter does not produce a harvest. **His order reveals the importance of timing and the sequence of life's events.** Walking in purpose, led by grace, resting in His order brings us to a place to truly understand and

His Order

appreciate stewardship. The world's view and popular teaching on stewardship is to care for another's property like it was your own. The lens of grace reveals that stewardship is taking care of what you've been given, but it is yours and His. Romans 11:36 says "For all things are His, through Him, to Him." This lesson is illustrated in the parable of the prodigal son. The son that stayed actually owned everything even though he did not realize it. True stewardship brings us to a place where we believe God and use all things for His glory, which is always our blessing. It is through our relationship He gives us all things. These are for us and the people around us and for God's glory to shine in it. I hope you are seeing the waltz of purpose, order, and stewardship. You cannot dance alone. The beauty of His glory is revealed when you dance with Him.

You can never give with a motive to get - that is manipulation and has nothing to do with God. Selfishness quenches the Spirit but few recognize His presence pulling back.

Jesus' prayers were heard because of His reverent submission (Hebrews 5:7). What if people aren't in reverent submission? What if they (self) have not submitted to God? Would it be safe to say due to the lack of reverent submission they are not heard? That's sobering and certainly explains a lot about the periods of silence. The dictionary defines Bias as a particular tendency, trend, inclination, feeling, or opinion, especially one that is preconceived or unreasoned. Bias, simply, is self-serving.

God, who is Love, is not self-seeking (1 For 13). When your motive is love then the world around you is getting a glimpse of God (not you). This brings Him glory.

TEACHING POINTS:
- First the spirit then the natural; God's order. God is first, not self.
- Where the mind goes, the body follows.
- His order reveals the importance of timing and sequence.
- Faith springs from hope and love and always produces action.
- Anxiety is from being in conflict with God's order.
- Most dismiss what they need because they can't "see" it leads to what they want.
- **What you do with what you've been given is stewardship**, think about the prodigal son.
- Waltz of purpose, order, and stewardship.
- A trap is seeking the things of God, even the ways of God, more than seeking intimate relationship with God who gives us all things.
- Bias is self-serving and leads people to make decisions that quenches the Spirit and leads to dryness of life.
- **When your motive is love then the world around you is getting a glimpse of God (not you).**
- Love well and God will live through you well and you will thrive in life (1 Jn 4:16).

DISCUSSION:
- Seedtime and harvest, summer and winter; God's order.

His Order

- Order consists of timing and sequence.
- Faith springs from hope and love and always produces action.
- Anxiety is not a result of the path of peace.
- Most want easy over the path of life; what they need.
- **What you do with what you've been given is stewardship**, good or bad.
- Partnership with God is like a Waltz.
- Relationship with God is key. It is He who gives us all things.
- Bias is self-serving and quenches the Spirit.
- **When your motive is love then the world around you is getting a glimpse of God (not you).**

ACTIVATION:
Join with the Holy Spirit this week and ask Him to help you love those in your path like Jesus does, not self-seeking, but trusting God has all you need and is using you to display His loving goodness.

SCRIPTURE REFERENCES:
"By faith we understand that the universe was formed at God's command, so that what is seen was not made out of what was visible."
- Hebrews 11:3

"He must manage his own family well and see that his children obey him with proper respect. 5(If anyone does not know how to manage his own family, how can he take care of God's church?)"
- 1 Timothy 3:4-5

The Purple Pill Book Study

"But seek first his kingdom and his righteousness, and all these things will be given to you as well."
- Matthew 6:33

"By faith the people passed through the Red SeaF50 as on dry land; but when the Egyptians tried to do so, they were drowned."
- Hebrews 11:29

"Being confident of this, that he who began a good work in you will carry it on to completion until the day of Christ Jesus."
- Philippians 1:6

"The LORD had said to Abram, "Leave your country, your people and your father's household and go to the land I will show you."
- Genesis 12:1

"He who dwells in the shelter of the Most High will rest in the shadow of the Almighty."
- Psalms 91:1

"A man came from Baal Shalishah, bringing the man of God twenty loaves of barley bread baked from the first ripe grain, along with some heads of new grain. "Give it to the people to eat," Elisha said. "How can I set this before a hundred men?" his servant asked. But Elisha answered, "Give it to the people to eat. For this is what the LORD says: 'They will eat and have some left over.' " Then he set it before them, and they ate and had some left over, according to the word of the LORD."

- 2 Kings 4:42-44

"Whoever does not love does not know God, because God is love."
- 1 John 4:8

"It (love) is not rude, it is not self-seeking, it is not easily angered, it keeps no record of wrongs."
- 1 Corinthians 13:5

"During the days of Jesus' life on earth, he offered up prayers and petitions with loud cries and tears to the one who could save him from death, and he was heard because of his reverent submission."
- Hebrews 5:7

"And so we know and rely on the love God has for us. God is love. Whoever lives in love lives in God, and God in him."
- 1 John 4:16

Eleven

His Kingdom

> **"THE church is not a building but the ecclesia, the called-out ones, to govern with a heart of love and bring order to earth."**

OVERVIEW Chapter 11 - His Kingdom
A Kingdom represents the king's rule, authority, will, and desires. Jesus introduced the gospel of the Kingdom here on earth and assigned us to go and make disciples of all nations that His Kingdom may come, and His will be done right here on earth, as it is in Heaven. God's Kingdom brings with it His rule, authority, and will. We usher in His Kingdom by bringing His freedom, grace, and love to the people that submit to His authority. Christ in us, the hope of glory, earmarks us as the stronger man that can come in and plunder a strongman who has kept people in bondage and set them free from the dominion of darkness, now living in the glorious light of His gospel of the Kingdom. This results in righteousness, joy, and peace. Wherever we go we usher in His Kingdom which is our greatest blessing and His greatest glory!

Love: The Key to the Kingdom
Love is the key to the Kingdom. Faith works by love

His Kingdom

(Galatians 4:6). Before divine promotion we find love - love for God, and love for yourself - this empowers you to love others. Partnering with God on our sojourn we find our job is to be faithful and live a life of love. Love God and love your neighbor like yourself. This is a place of rest. This is not a formula or list of endless tasks that drain the life out of you. This is life with God, full of joy, peace, and all of the wonderful fruit of the Spirit. Resting in what He has done and availed to us by His grace.

Love is a spirit and unleashes God's power. This is a process that never ends, but if you do not play your part - live a life of love - then the process stalls and you are repeatedly presented with one opportunity to love after another.

The sower sows the word. I remind you that Jesus is the living word (John 1), and God is love (1 John 4:8). **Sowing the word therefore is sowing love.** To produce a crop, it must find good soil - your heart must be a heart where love may flourish. You want a theology that empowers you as the world is shaken and trouble increases. You are not here to escape to heaven. Jesus had authority in heaven, authority on earth, and authority in hell. His kingdom in heaven was brought to earth. He came as a man to set us free to walk in our God given authority free from sin and darkness. **You are here to bring His Kingdom of love to the earth.** You are here to prepare Jesus' inheritance of people and nations on earth. Heaven on earth. The gospel of the Kingdom releases you to be at the epicenter of all culture that we might shine with God's love and bring heaven to earth. The church is not a building but the ecclesia, the called-out ones, to govern with a heart of love and bring order to earth.

TEACHING POINTS:
- The Kingdom represents the King's rules, heart, and dominion.
- God is Love and His Kingdom is a one of LOVE.
- Sowing the Word is sowing Love.
- Your destiny aligns with bringing His Kingdom of Love to earth.
- We don't practice a formula but live a life of love; love for God, our neighbors, and ourselves.

DISCUSSION:
- To successfully press through transition to find promotion is only correctly done through our partnership with God.
- Pre-requisites to promotion are Faith, Hope, and Love.
- Without faith you cannot please God.
- Faith cannot exist without hope.
- Love God and love your neighbor like yourself, is a place of rest, not a formula.
- God is love.

ACTIVATION:
"Rule with the heart of a servant, and serve with the heart of king." -Pastor Bill Johnson

SCRIPTURE REFERENCES:
"And without faith it is impossible to please God, because anyone who comes to him must believe that he exists and that he rewards those who earnestly seek him."

- Hebrews 11:6

"Without weakening in his faith, he faced the fact that his body was as good as dead—since he was about a hundred years old—and that Sarah's womb was also dead. Yet he did not waver through unbelief regarding the promise of God, but was strengthened in his faith and gave glory to God."
- Romans 4:19-20

"Now faith is being sure of what we hope for and certain of what we do not see."
- Hebrews 11:1

"Whoever does not love does not know God, because God is love."
- 1 John 4:8

Handouts

Twelve

Declarations of Life

I am [your name] and I declare:

Who I am
I love the lord with all my Heart, soul, and strength (Lk 10:27)
I am a child of the most high God (1 Jn 3:1)
As for me and my house we will serve the lord! (Joshua 24:15)
I dwell in the secret place of the most high. I rest in the shadow of the almighty (Ps 91:1)
He is my refuge, my fortress, my God in whom I trust. (Ps 91:2)
I am born again by the blood of Jesus (1 Pet 1:19-23)
God takes me into his confidence (Pr 3:32)
God is pleased to have all his fullness dwell in me (col 1:19)
I am an oracle of God (1 Pet 4:11)
The lord has done great things for me and I am filled with joy! (Ps 126:3)
He teaches me the way I should go, and He counsels and watches over me. (Ps 32:8)
God loves me and his unfailing love surrounds me! (1 Jn 4:16 and Jn 3:16 and Ps 32:10)

The same spirit that raised Christ from the dead lives in me! (Ro 8:11)
Christ lives in me, the hope of glory (col 1:27)
God almighty beautifies, dignifies and crowns me with loving-kindness and tender mercy (Ps 103:4)
The Lord guides me always, satisfies my needs, and strengthens my frame. I am like a well-watered garden, like a spring whose waters never fail!!! (Is 58:11)
I bring living water to dry ground, wherever I go life springs up (Is 44:3-4, Jn 4, Jn 14:12)
I am a minister of reconciliation (2 Cor 5:18)
I bring good news (Mt 4:23 and Mk 16:15)
I know all things (1 Jn 2:20)
I Hear counsel, receive instruction, and accept correction, that I may be wise in the time to come. (Pr 19:20)
I am crowned with knowledge (Pr 14:18)
My wife is beautiful, she's wise, understanding, and Prudent - a gift from the Lord! (Pr 19:14)

Healing
I am Healed by the stripes of Jesus (1 Pet 2:24 and is 53:5)
I bless the Lord and forget not all his benefits (Ps 103:2)
He Heals all my diseases and redeems my life from the pit (Ps 103:3-4)
Jehovah Rapha, the Lord that Heals me, lives in me (Ex 15:26 Ro 8:11)
He sent his word and Healed me (Ps 107:20)
His word is life and Health to my whole body! (Pr 4:22)

My tongue is a tree of life and brings healing. (Pr 15:4)
I lay hands on the sick and they recover (Mk 16:18)
I trust in the Lord with all my heart and lean not on my own understanding, in all my ways I acknowledge him and He makes my paths straight, I am not wise in my own eyes, I fear the Lord and shun evil. This brings health to my body and nourishment to my bones. (Pr 3:5-8)

Prosperity
I honor the Lord with my wealth, with the first fruits of all my crops, then my barns are filled to overflowing and my vats brim over with new wine! (Pr 3:9-10)
God has plans to prosper me, to give me hope and a good future (Jer 29:11)
God gives sinners the task of gathering and storing up wealth to hand it over to me, the man of faith. (Ecc 2:26)
God bestows favor and honor on me and withholds no good thing from me (Ps 84:11)
I magnify the Lord and He takes pleasure in my prosperity (Ps 35:27)
God gives me the power to create wealth to establish his covenant on the earth (Dt 8:18)
I am blessed when I come in and I am blessed when I go out (Dt 28:6)
His blessing brings wealth and He adds no trouble to it. (Pr 10:22)
The Lord grants me abundant prosperity (Dt 28:11 and Pr 21:21)
I will lend to many but will borrow from none. (Dt

Declarations of Life

28:12c)
Everything I put my hand to prospers (Dt 28:8)
God brings increase to me and my children (Ps 115:14 and Gen 1:28)
My children will be mighty in the land (Ps 112:2)
I train my children in the way they should go and they never turn from it (Pr 22:6)
All of his blessings will chase me down and overtake me (Dt 28:2)
His favor is a shield about me (Ps 5:12)
He supplies all my needs according to his riches (Phil 4:19)
I am an oak of righteousness planted by the Lord, my leaf does not wither, whatever I do prospers (Is 61:4. Ps 1:3)

Authority
I am a man under authority (Mt 8:9, 1 Pet 2:13)
I have been given authority over all the power of darkness. (Eph 1:21 and 2:6 Mk 16:17)
I am seated with Christ in the Heavenlies far above all rule, power, and dominion (Eph 2:6)
I am anointed, have his seal of ownership; His Spirit in me (2 Cor 1:21-22)
The Spirit of the Lord is upon me; to bring good news of his Kingdom, proclaim freedom for the captives, the blind see, the deaf hear, the lame walk, this is the year of the Lord's favor (Lk 4:18-19)

Righteousness
I am the righteousness of God in Christ Jesus (2 Cor 5:21)
I am dead to sin (Ro 6:11,14 and 1 Pet 2:24)

I am alive to righteousness (1 Pet 2:24)
I have the mind of Christ! (1 Cor 2:16)

Divine Protection
No harm, will come near me, my family, or my dwellings (Pr 12:21)
His angels watch over me and carry out his word (Ps 103:20)
God is my Help, my shield, and my very great reward! (Ps 115:11, 1 Pet 1:5, Gen 15:1)
I will never be shaken and I have no fear (Ps 112:6, 8, and Is 54:14)
God has victory in store for me, and He guards my course and protects my way (Pr 2:8)
No weapon forged against me will prosper. (Is 54:17)
I will refute every tongue that accuses me. (Is 54:17)
An enemy may come at me in one direction but He will flee from me in seven directions. (Dt 28:7)
God has victory in store for me. (Pr 2:7)
My steps are not hampered and my foot is not snared (Pr 4:12 and 3:26)

Faith
I live by faith in the son of God. (Gal 2:20)
I do not merely listen to the word, and deceive myself, I do what it says!!! (Ja 1:22)
I believe and therefore I speak (2 Cor 4:13)
My tongue has the power of life and death and I speak life! (Pr 18:21)
His word is truth (Jn 17:17)

His word is eternal (Mt 24:35)
What I see in the physical is temporary (2 Cor 4:18)
I walk by faith not by sight (2 Cor 5:7)
I am sure of what I hope for and certain of what I do not see. (Heb 11:1)
God gives life to the dead and calls things that are not as though they were! (Ro 4:17)
I am a believer (Mk 16:17)
All of his promises are yes for me and I speak the amen for his glory (2 Cor 1:20)
Every word of God contains the power to be fulfilled! (Lk 1:37)
My Heart is good soil and his word produces a crop of a hundredfold! (Lk 8:15)
I have been set free from the law of sin and death
I live by the law of the spirit of life (Ro 8:2)

Wisdom
God gives me wisdom and from his mouth comes knowledge and understanding (Pr 2:6)
He gives me wisdom, knowledge and joy. (Ecc 2:26)
Wisdom sets a garland of grace on my head and presents me with a crown of splendor (Pr 4:9)
Wisdom is my sister and understanding my kinsman. (Pr 7:4)
Wisdom speaks what is true (Pr 8:7)
Wisdom is more precious than rubies nothing I desire can compare with Her! (Pr 8:11)
Wisdom has understanding and power, riches, honor, enduring wealth, and prosperity (Pr 8:14 8:18)
She bestows wealth on those who love Her, making

their treasuries full.   (Pr 8:21)
Wisdom is supreme; therefore, I get wisdom! (Pr 4:7)

I am filled with the holy spirit (Acts 2:4 and 13:52)
The same spirit that raised Christ from the dead lives in me (Ro 8:11)
All the fullness of Christ lives in my flesh.   (Col 2:10)
God gives me wisdom and revelation to know him and his incomparably great power! (Eph 1:17-19)
I have the ever-increasing fruit of the spirit; love, joy, peace, patience, kindness, goodness, faithfulness, gentleness, and self-control. (Gal 5:22-25)
I have his peace and follow the path of peace (Jn 14:27 and Col 3:15)

He took my sin and gave me his righteousness (1 Pet 2:24)
He took my sickness and gave me Health (1 Pet 2:24)
He took my poverty and gave me prosperity (2 Cor 8:9)
He took death and gave me life and life in abundance!

God is good, all of the time!!! (Ro 12:2)
For not one word of his promises has failed! (1 Kings 8:56)
Praise the Lord, praise His holy name, thank you Father for all of your blessings!!!   (Eph 1:3)

The Purple Pill Workbook
God's call for His bride to make herself ready.

Copyright © 2018 Robert E. Statham

Author Page

Rob's a reputation for prophetic insight and revelation brings living water to dry ground. Along the lines of Gideon, he believes many others are more qualified to share God's heart, but once again God chooses the weak and foolish things to bring His heart's desire to earth.

The best way to contact Rob is by email rob@robstatham.com or twitter @RobertEStatham.

Thank you for reading The Purple Pill with the workbook. We love feedback. Please leave a review on Amazon when it's convenient.

May God bless and prosper you abundantly so the whole world may see God's glory.

www.ingramcontent.com/pod-product-compliance
Lightning Source LLC
Chambersburg PA
CBHW030456010526
44118CB00011B/965